Baitz, Jon Robin,
1961-
    Other desert cities

Other Desert Cities

By the same author

Plays
Mizlansky/Zilinsky or, Schmucks
The Film Society
The Substance of Fire
The End of the Day
Three Hotels
A Fair Country
Ten Unknowns
Chinese Friends
The Paris Letter
My Beautiful Goddamn City

Adaptation of *Hedda Gabler* by Hebrik Ibsen

Screenplays
The Substance of Fire
People I Know

JON ROBIN BAITZ

Other Desert Cities

A Play in Two Acts

Introduction by Honor Moore

Grove Press
New York

INTRODUCTION

A daughter returns home for Christmas for the first time in years, bearing the manuscript of a memoir, which reveals a devastating episode in the life of her wealthy Republican family. Her beloved older brother, eldest child of the family in question, was involved in a radical group in the 1970s that bombed a draft center; the explosion killed a man and brought about the brother's suicide. The events, years in the past at the time of the play, emotionally ravaged the daughter; disturbed the upbringing of the younger son, a child when the events happened; opened a schism between the mother and her sister; and shattered the orderly lives of the parents, causing their ostracism from an intimate circle of friends, which included President and Mrs. Reagan.

It was millennia ago that the first actor stood forward from the chorus and the theatre began. In outdoor arenas seating thousands, ancient communities worked out tragedies and contradictions. Think of *The Trojan Women* of Euripides, in which women in the ruling family of a conquered nation mourn their husbands and sons who died there; of *Lysistrata,* in which Aristophanes depicts an antiwar sex strike by the women of Athens; of *Antigone,* in which a daughter battles to give her brother a proper burial. These great plays constructed stories that held their audiences in thrall long enough to affect their emotions, to change their attitudes—the original meaning of "catharsis" was "purification."

As the novel was the product of the rise of the bourgeoisie, so the contemporary memoir is a direct consequence of the revolution that disrupted American cultural life in the 1970s when African American writers, women writers, gay writers, and other non-white or minority writers began to publish, in numbers, the stories of our lives. We wished to speak our own realities rather than allow ourselves to be characterized only by (mostly) white and male writers—and we began to speak in memoir. Though fiction and poetry by these formerly outsider populations also moved decisively into the mainstream, it was memoir that flourished, as if fiction might distort reality and the canvas of poetry were insufficiently vast.

Four decades on, the genre whose origins I mark at the publication in 1974 of Maxine Hong Kingston's *The Woman Warrior,* is still threatening enough to inspire jeers; recently, in the book review of record, a critic, assessing four memoirs, concluded that in the presence of so many inferior examples, prospective memoirists might "take a break." Why me? asks the memoirist. Every year thousands of novels and books of poems of debatable quality appear right alongside those considered great or at least good, and no one calls for a moratorium.

Such battles are nothing new in the history of literature, but no literary movement since the Modernists banished the metric line has brought on such conflict. In the last few years, when certain memoirs have been exposed as invention, reports on the perfidy of autobiographical writers have raged across front pages, as if something akin to murder had been committed. Since when have human beings not told lies? Since when have there not been literary hoaxes? Could it be that the intensity of the ruckus has less to do with the prevarication of a few authors, than with cultural resistance to the truths memoirs continue to reveal?

Change is not comfortable, neither is the most influential literature. Every time a truth formerly withheld bursts into view, the dynamics of society alter a little, freeing stories already lived and expanding the range of stories it will be possible to live in the future. Employing dramaturgy, which draws on Greek tragedy (the returning daughter), boulevard comedy (the play is funny), and Arthur Miller tragedy (children challenge their parents' integrity), Jon Robin Baitz meticulously unpacks all the ethical dilemmas of the present controversy while constructing a play that turns on the revelation of a truly surprising secret, just like a great memoir. Evenhanded, but never sacrificing a commitment to the truth or to the emotions that bind a family, Baitz allows all the important questions to be asked. When a family is involved, who owns the story? What kind of consequences might require a writer to have a responsibility beyond herself and her commitment to her art? When is the publication of "just a book" worth the splintering of a family?

What is a writer talking about when she says that telling her story is for her "a matter of life and death." Is there any such thing as a secret that should be kept?

As the play unfolds, the making of art—in this case the publication of a book—becomes a metaphor for the investigation of the cost of telling of truth inside one particular family. At the same time, a contemporary dramatist reveals to us that we are in the midst of a cultural shift that challenges us to a higher standard of ethics, to greater courage and honesty in that first society where we all begin our lives, the family. I was not the only one in tears when the lights dimmed after the last scene. No one could stop clapping. What a relief, I thought to myself as I walked out into the snowy night. I am not alone after all.

—Honor Moore
New York City, 2011

Other Desert Cities had its world premier at Lincoln Center Theater (under the direction of André Bishop, Artistic Director, and Bernard Gersten, Executive Producer) at the Mitzi E. Newhouse Theater, New York, NY, on December 16, 2010, and officially opened on January 13, 2011. It was directed by Joe Mantello; set design was by John Lee Beatty; costume design by David Zinn; lighting design by Kenneth Posner; sound design by Jill BC Du Boff; and original music composed by Justin Ellington. The cast was as follows:

BROOKE WYETH Elizabeth Marvel
POLLY WYETH Stockard Channing
LYMAN WYETH Stacey Keach
SILDA GRAUMAN Linda Lavin
TRIP WYETH Thomas Sadowksi

Other Desert Cities then had its Broadway premier at the Booth Theatre, New York, NY, on October 12, 2011, and officially opened on November 3, 2011. It was directed by Joe Mantello; set design was by John Lee Beatty; costume design by David Zinn; lighting design by Kenneth Posner; sound design by Jill BC Du Boff; and original music composed by Justin Ellington. The cast was as follows:

BROOKE WYETH Rachel Griffiths
POLLY WYETH Stockard Channing
LYMAN WYETH Stacey Keach
SILDA GRAUMAN Judith Light
TRIP WYETH Thomas Sadowksi

for André Bishop and Joe Mantello; two men of the theatre
who kept the lights on and drew the maps for me.

and for

Gordon Davidson and Sir David Hare,
both of whom make me want to read, watch, and write plays.

ACT I

The Wyeth living room. There is a metal fireplace, one of those Scandinavian flying saucer types from the sixties, giving off a nice glow. Desert-French regency is the style, decorated for movie stars circa 1965, but somehow it still works, perhaps better now than it did in its time.

A game of mixed doubles has just ended. BROOKE WYETH, *an attractive and dry woman, her oak-like father,* LYMAN, *who is sturdy in the way of old Californians of a particular type. Brook's younger brother,* TRIP, *a bright, funny man, perhaps a decade her junior, and her mother, elegant and forthright and whip-smart* POLLY. *They are still tired, recovering from the game. In easy, good spirits.*

POLLY All I am saying Brooke is that I don't know how the hell you stand those East Coast winters, and in that little village of yours out there on the edge of the sea, it's just, it really makes us worry—

BROOKE *(laughing)* Sag Harbor is really cozy, it's quiet, it's peaceful, my God, I've been here less than three hours and you're starting in on me? About where I live?

LYMAN What your mother is saying is that closer to home—we would love to have you closer to home—

TRIP I can't believe you're doing this. Mom, Dad—she *split*. She gave up on California, last century. It's *not in her blood.*

BROOKE It really is true, even when I was a little girl, I knew, I just knew I was going to live back east. I couldn't do this—this endless sunshine—this—it's so—predictable!

LYMAN But you're a child of California, you grew up with beaches and orange groves—

BROOKE And the weather that never changes. I need *seasons* to mark where I am. Last winter I was still pretty blue, as you know, but this odd thing—when spring started to just hint—those crazy flowers popping up out of the snow—it matched where I was, *I* was coming out of it. My winter. I was popping up too.

A moment.

POLLY I think you might have that thing where the winter is part of what makes you blue, really, have you ever thought of that?

BROOKE I am *fine*, I'm—is this what this trip is gonna be?

TRIP Brooke. The house next door? It's for sale. They want us to have it. *(mock horror)* They want us here ALL THE TIME!

Trip pretends to be dying of poison gas. The parents grin. Brooke laughs.

LYMAN Yes, we know we bore you two to tears. But . . . *(beat)* Brookie. What if there were another attack? It's a rather likely possibility, isn't it? It's only been a few years. It's only been—I mean—

BROOKE *(moaning)*	**TRIP**
Here we go.	No, no, no. Let's not do this.

POLLY You know, we still have friends in Washington, you wouldn't believe what they don't tell you. Well, *we* hear it, blood chilling. Arabs with all sorts of plans they're hatching, crazed Indian people with—

BROOKE I live in Eastern Long Island, not Times Square, and I refuse to live like some sort of terrified—*(beat)* This is how you win at tennis, you agitate me—you get me really just—impossibly overheated—

2

POLLY   I have *no* idea what you're talking about. If you have a lousy serve, you have a lousy serve, darling, and if all it takes to win is to tell you that I think this war is entirely justified, well then, you shouldn't be playing tennis.

Polly has a smile on her face. She is having fun, it's light needling.

BROOKE *(grinning)*   Do you still own a revolver, dad?

POLLY   You know I'm not cooking dinner? We're having Christmas Eve at the country club.

Brooke lets out a moan.

TRIP   Jesus, Mom, who has Christmas at a country club?

BROOKE   Jews is who has Christmas at a country club. That's why God made country clubs, so half-goy hipsters and their aging parents don't have to cook.

POLLY   Oh, it's terrific. Stone crab claws, Bloody Marys, chink food, and a mambo band. If you want to stand here slaving over a hot stove in the desert, be my guest. I can't face it anymore.

BROOKE *(smiling)*   Did you just say 'chink food'? Cause I'm still stuck back there.

POLLY *(laughing)*   Oh stop it! I don't have a bigoted bone in my body, you're just so correct about everything, and if you can't joke in your own home—you're so—I wanna know this; when did everyone get so damn sensitive about every last thing? When?

BROOKE   Uhm. Around the time you people started using words like "chink" in public, is when.

LYMAN   You don't like the Palm Springs Country Club? Is there anything about our lives you don't mind? Our politics, our—

BROOKE *(over him)*   That country club does not let in—

POLLY *(over her)*   Yes they do. Yes they DO! That ended *years* ago! Stop it!

3

BROOKE *Do they?* Mom? How many—

POLLY Most of the club is! Now. Believe me, I should know!

BROOKE Really, please stop talking about it like it's temple Beth Shalom.

LYMAN It's a great place, and by the way, we heard Colin Powell lecture there last month and if he's behind the war, you can trust it's the right thing to do. He knows *a lot* more than you do, Brooke. Most trusted man in America.

Brooke is about to counter this statement, and is halted by Trip.

TRIP Look; we talk politics, it's only eight in the morning, the whole day will be shot to shit, really. It will just dissolve into stiff upper-lipped thermonuclear family war.

LYMAN *(grinning)* Can't have that, can we? Look: despite your abhorrent and repugnant lefty politics, we want you to know we're *damn* proud of you.

BROOKE Proud? What did I do?

LYMAN Brooke. C'mon. Your book. You sold it to the first people who read it.

POLLY Which is a great relief as you will no longer be known as the girl who had only one novel in her.

BROOKE *(bursts out laughing)* Well, I didn't realize I *was!*

POLLY Oh come on, dear, after six years, everyone was beginning to wonder. You did *bring* it, didn't you?

Beat.

BROOKE Yeah, but I have to make copies in town, I wasn't going to carry a bunch of copies on the plane.

POLLY We got the craziest call. Someone's doing a vulgar little picture book on old Hollywood nightlife, and they heard we had lots of pictures from Chasen's and the Brown Derby and Ron

4

and Nancy. I said I would be saving them in case I decided to do a book of my own, which I can assure you, I will not. *(drinking water)* This water needs vodka for flavor.

Lyman picks up the Los Angeles Times.

LYMAN *(reading)*   Huh. Look at this: Don Rumsfeld is paying a visit to the troops in Baghdad.

POLLY   Isn't that a nice thoughtful Christmas present.

BROOKE   Maybe while he's out in the desert he can dig up some of them weapons of mass destruction—

TRIP *(over her)*   NO! No! *No discussion of the war.* This is a cardinal goddamn rule—we'll be here all day, and I want to get back in time so you can see my show.

He has a sly smile on his face. She looks at him, caught.

BROOKE   I told you it won't really mean anything to me, I don't *watch* television—

TRIP   Well, unless you've suddenly become Amish, that's unbelievably pretentious.

LYMAN *(grinning)*   Oh, Brooke, you really *have* to see it.

POLLY   It's quite extraordinary really. You've never seen anything quite like it.

BROOKE   I don't understand even the *premise.* It's like a court room thing with a—?

POLLY *(relishing this)*   Oh, I can explain. You see—this is what your brother's talents and education have led him to, Brooke: a fake TV courtroom with fake trials featuring roving litigants out to make a buck.

TRIP   Hey! *Jury of Your Peers* is a huge hit. It's not fake!

LYMAN   That man is a *real judge?*

TRIP He's a retired judge from Encino. It's a regular trial, only, the jury is made up of stars.

POLLY Stars? Those are not stars! Gary Cooper was a star! These are what appear to be some very moth-eaten, down-on-their luck has-beens.

TRIP *(to Brooke)* Who basically—you know—roast both the—it's very funny—both the defendant and the plaintiff—and render a verdict. And if some of them are midgets, well, why not?

LYMAN *Please!* This is how the law is conducted in this country now? A freak show with carnies making mock.

TRIP Dad, come on, it's *show biz*. Everyone signs a waiver, it's civil court, the show pays.

LYMAN *Oh,* so there's no harm, no foul, no matter how wrong the person is, the show pays! What is the name of the judge?

TRIP *(trying not to laugh, looking down)* Uhm. Him? He's uh, well, yeah, his name is Judge Myron C. Glimmelman.

The three of them stand there, saying nothing. Polly stifles a derisive snort. Brooke is grinning madly, waiting. Shaking her head.

POLLY *(shakes her head)* Oh, my people, my people, my people.

TRIP *(a smile)* He is a great guy! All moral rectitude and good hair.

BROOKE Just like you, Daddy.

LYMAN *(playing straight man)* I would never sell myself like some common—

BROOKE *(laughing over him)* Oh really? Mr. Ambassador?

TRIP Respectfully, what was being the spokesman for the California Wine Board?

LYMAN Public service, something you know nothing about—

TRIP *(ala his dad, stentorian)* "Drink in the wines—

TRIP/LYMAN —of the Golden State, and taste how the west was won."

There is laughter. This is an old bit.

LYMAN We were trying to promote the state's growing—

BROOKE *(over him)* And let's not forget some of those *movies* you were in before you sold out and became a politician.

LYMAN *(laughs)* I did not sell out, I found a higher calling, you ungrateful little brat!

TRIP Hey. People need to laugh today. It's all so serious and goddamn, you know, *horrible* out there. We could all get anthraxed any minute—people need a laugh!

POLLY It's our fault, Lyman, we failed at providing normalcy— we had two children, and both of them have entirely abnormal careers . . .

BROOKE *(cuts her off, tense)* Three, actually.

POLLY Excuse me?

There is a moment.

BROOKE Three children.

Beat.

POLLY Three. Of course.

A slight tension, which Lyman labors to climb over.

LYMAN So, Trip, you're basically saying that being *right or wrong* matters a lot less than being *funny.*

TRIP *Funny* is all we have left. Yes! *They flew planes into buildings!* People *need* funny. I can't argue with you about this, if you fail to see the merit in what I do, that's your loss, all of you. We can't all be hopelessly highbrow like Brooke, some of us have to actually make money. I'm gonna take a shower. Breakfast on me.

He leaves.

LYMAN   What does he mean, 'people flew planes into buildings?' What's that got to do with *Jury of Your Peers*?

BROOKE   Hey—Should we wake Aunt Silda, is she joining us for breakfast?

POLLY   My sister seems to be sleeping 'til noon or so, at least. Ever since she came back from rehab she stays up all night watching old movies.

BROOKE   Why did she slip? Do you know?

POLLY   Please. Who knows. She had been doing okay, you know, that's the thing, she had five years sobriety—and she went, just like that.

Polly snaps her fingers.

BROOKE   How bad is it? Exactly?

POLLY   The woman's liver needs a liver.

BROOKE   Owww. So. She's going to live here? With you.

Beat. Polly looks at Lyman and shakes her head in defeat.

LYMAN   Yes. I insisted.

POLLY   *Not forever.* Only for a bit, 'til she's back on her feet and we know she's not going to slip.

BROOKE   I think she's very lucky to have you looking after her.

POLLY   Well, she's not getting the same level of care we gave you, believe me. *(beat)* You're getting your old glow back. See how good it is for you to be out here, darling?

BROOKE *(laughing)*   I am *NOT* moving in *next door*, forget it!

Lyman smiles.

LYMAN It's nice to see you happy, lighter, you seem lighter. Which is very important to us.

POLLY To have lightness. I would say nothing is quite as important.

BROOKE Lightness is good.

LYMAN Yes. And health.

POLLY My knees, thank God, it was bone on bone for years, which is why I was such a bitch through the nineties.

BROOKE *(grinning)* That's why, Mom? Your *knees?* Oh. It was your "knees" that made you so very quarrelsome. And what was it in the seventies? Had I known it was your body . . .

POLLY I think living on the East Coast has given you the impression that sarcasm is alluring and charming. It is not. Sarcasm is the purview of teenagers and homosexuals.

BROOKE Now that I'm single, those are basically my two preferred social groups, so . . .

POLLY Yes. We got a letter from Cary, telling us he always loved us and he hoped we would still consider him family.

BROOKE *(a sigh)* Please don't. He's not family.

POLLY You quit the marriage counseling?

BROOKE Well, I mean, *yes,* it seemed the best idea after Cary stopped *showing up.*

POLLY Did you badger him or something?

LYMAN Polly.

BROOKE Mom. Mom. Jesus. He's in London.

POLLY When did he leave?

BROOKE Two months ago. Three. Four.

POLLY And you didn't *tell* us?

9

BROOKE *(laughing, exhausted)* Look. *It's over,* Mom. It's been over since it *began,* really. We had a decent run, three years in marriage these days is like twenty when you guys were kids.

LYMAN We hate you being alone.

BROOKE I *love* me being alone.

POLLY If you could just find someone like your brother, funny and fun.

BROOKE *(a burst of laughter)* Like *Trip Wyeth?* The ADD riddled, junk-food-addicted porn-surfing Trip Wyeth, my little brother?

POLLY He is not addicted to junk food; he eats very well. The porn, I suppose, I will give you. I mean—someone younger. Cary was too old. Too old and too British, which is the same thing, really. They're all so old, the Brits, even the children. You need someone zippy.

BROOKE *(laughing)* "Someone zippy?"

POLLY Find someone peppy and youthful. These days, the age difference means nothing. Lyman, apparently it's very hip, very 'with-it' for older women to have younger men. Much younger.

BROOKE Stop worrying! I'm *fine.* Now I'm really hungry, can we go? Can we just for the love of God, go get *breakfast?*

POLLY Yes, yes, fine. I'm going to go get dressed. If you twist my arm, Brooke, we could stop at Saks; because you are never going to meet *anyone* if you continue to dress like a refugee from a library in Kabul.

BROOKE *(looks at herself)* I'm wearing tennis clothes! To play *tennis* in!

Polly leaves with her glass, leaving Brooke and Lyman alone.

LYMAN Do you have a smoke, we could go outside and sneak?

BROOKE Not on my person, Daddy. I thought you quit?

LYMAN I did, it's fun to sneak them. Your mother sneaks them too, it's a little game we have. We steal each other's smokes. It is amazing really, what you do to entertain yourself in the desert.

BROOKE I have pot for later.

LYMAN Are you allowed to smoke pot with the antidepressants?

BROOKE Oh, sure, but only with a gin chaser.

LYMAN It's not funny, Brooke. It's really not. You're supposed to be careful. Damn it. Really.

BROOKE One of the nice myths about pain is that one apparently can't literally remember it. Which is why women have more than one child. Well, Daddy, I'm here to tell you, I have a very good memory for pain.

LYMAN I wrote you last month offering money.

BROOKE Yes. You did.

LYMAN You have not favored me with the courtesy of a reply.

BROOKE Daddy. I don't need your money—my life works. Just as it is. Simple. Clean.

LYMAN But why not? Given how tenuous things are getting—I want only to make your life at least incrementally—

BROOKE *(laughing)* Better? Money does that—how? Has it—ever—for us? No. We all know that much by now. I am pleading with you, don't make this whole trip about a check from you. Okay?

LYMAN What kind of living do you make? Those magazine pieces? Oh, it's very nice when *Gourmet* or *Travel and Leisure* sends you to Sri Lanka, and god knows what you get for an editorial—but at the end of the day? It's hand to mouth.

BROOKE Dad, all my friends who get a check from home—there is not a single one of them—not one—whom it has not crippled in some fundamental way. I have everything I need. Really, please. The balance is so delicate, I can't screw with it.

LYMAN What if it happens again? A depression? You lost—you lost *years*—we watched, helpless—that hospital.

BROOKE Look—I take the lovely little pills, and I see the blessed Doctor Leighton every week, twice a week, and I do yoga, and I eat right, and I have learned optimism just like the magazines told us to. And now I know how to handle it.

LYMAN I'm sorry.

BROOKE Daddy, look at me. I've had tough times and everything that has happened to me—everything—has made me stronger. I'm your child. And mom's. Two old trees. Two old oak trees. And I'm an oak, too. Okay, got it? Oaks.

LYMAN We all have our ways of coping; mine is to be overprotective late in life. You sometimes seem to fail to understand that I lost a child. Therefore I am unable to relax about my remaining two.

BROOKE You can't live like that.

LYMAN It's collateral damage. I don't expect you could know what that feels like, my darling.

BROOKE *(quietly)* How can you say that. "I don't know what it feels like." I lost my older brother. He was my best friend—you know, I don't make friends easily, he was—most of my world and—then he was gone—

LYMAN You still miss him.

BROOKE Every day, most of the day, *all day*.

LYMAN *(a small, wan smile. An older smile. Plaintive.)* For me it's the holidays; at Christmas, I think of your brother. I think of Henry. Of what's left. Of time, and of everything. You'd think it would be forgotten by now.

BROOKE Just because you moved to the desert does not mean that anybody with a computer couldn't find out what happened with this family in a matter of moments. It's part of who we are, we can't just pretend it never happened.

LYMAN A lot of people get through the entirety of their lives, pretending; at a certain point, it's not the worst thing to do.

BROOKE I'm sorry, Daddy, I tried to live that way, and I just can't. I need to actually talk about it. Not in code, not obliquely, we have never . . .

LYMAN *(Pained. But sharp, shutting this down.)* I can't. *(He stops. Shakes his head. Softens.)* Maybe it's the old actor in me. Maybe I prefer my lines written down. Sometimes I see myself on the TV, late at night, grimacing with a forty-five in my hand, arresting someone. That was so much easier.

BROOKE *(a sad smile)* You should have stayed a movie star. You were so handsome.

LYMAN Yes, but it mortified me. I just looked good in a suit.

Polly appears in the doorway dressed in a bright caftan, and wearing bright jade earrings, a sort of David Hockney subject, posing.

POLLY *(calling out)* Well, let's get moving, I don't want to be stuck on Palm Canyon Drive in the noonday sun—all that last minute Christmas shopping, and at Saks those people spraying you with perfumes called "Maid's Night Out" or something. I still have some stuff to get . . . ! My hairdresser needs some Givenchy shower splash and a new wok.

She leaves.

BROOKE "Shower splash and a new wok." What else is there to life?

Lyman looks at Brooke, his face in a small wry smile, knowing, and melancholy.

LYMAN Oh, Brooke, you think everything is funny. Even when you were blue, the twinkle. But sometimes you can't help it, little girl and the twinkle isn't there.

Lyman exits. Brooke sits alone for a moment. Shaken at being seen so clearly by Lyman, despite her good cheer. She goes to her bag, takes out some pills, swallows them with water, and looks out.

Trip comes out, dressed in old Bermuda shorts and faded polo shirt, old tennis shoes, no socks.

TRIP *(grinning)* Ohh, you're already staring off into the desert; that's not good.

BROOKE *(still looking out)* You know that sign on the highway where you can either turn off for Palm Springs or keep going to "Other Desert Cities"? I am always so tempted just to keep on driving, you know. How do they *do* it? They never even leave anymore. They barely go into L.A.

TRIP Not barely enough—enough for me though: when they do come, I have to drop whatever I'm doing to meet them for dinner at some awful old restaurant with goddamn swans in Pasadena.

BROOKE The restaurant serves swan?

TRIP Shut up. You need tennis lessons, you've lost your game and your serve sucks, you used to be good at it.

BROOKE Well, I used to be good at a lot of things and the trouble with being good at things is that it takes too much work to *stay* good at them.

TRIP With that attitude it's a fucking *miracle* you finished your book.

BROOKE My book, my book, my book. What happens if they hate it?

TRIP They've never hated anything you've written.

BROOKE   I just get the sense that it's not gonna be so easy—I was kidding myself. It's so much pressure—

TRIP   Look, it's not like you've written some poor little Hollywood upbringing shit, is it?

BROOKE   No, but it *is* about Henry. Whom we can't talk about, it's about our brother, who went to war with our parents, joined a cult, disappeared, and then planted a bomb in an army recruiting station, before *killing* himself—is what it's actually *about*.

Pause. He takes this in.

TRIP   Okay, so maybe it won't be the recommendation for their Book of the Month Club. *(beat)* And he didn't 'plant' the bomb.

BROOKE   No. Maybe he didn't. But he was party to it. *(beat)* I mean, it's loving and I love them, and how can they see it as anything other than—

TRIP   Look, if you're scared of what they might say, I'll protect you, *relax*.

BROOKE   You can't protect me. Not from her. Not from Polly Wyeth.

TRIP   Oh yeah? You know what it takes to produce a TV show five nights a week? You have to have nerves of steel. It's as though having a show on the air turns people into that little creature with the ring in that stupid movie with those little assholes in the middle ages fighting elves and shit.

Brooke looks bewildered.

BROOKE   I um, literally have no idea what anything you just said means, literally.

TRIP *(flat)*   Literally: you don't know *Lord of the Rings*?

BROOKE   Literally, I have no idea.

TRIP   Shut up. you pretend to hate pop culture, but secretly you fucking love it. Why do you fight it? It's in our blood. Look at us. Look at dad! A gunslinger and a gumshoe at Paramount, and mom and Aunt Silda wrote those crazy-ass *Hilary* movies.

BROOKE *(laughing)*   Oh my God, *Hilary*! Over thanksgiving, I lay in bed, I had the flu or like consumption or something the whole time, I watched the DVD box set of all of them.

TRIP   There's a *box set*?

BROOKE   Yeah. From *Here Comes Hilary* to *Hasta La Vista Hilary*. They're *magnificent*.

TRIP   I never saw that last one.

BROOKE   Yeah, that's the best, and Mom was, OF COURSE, in a feud with Aunt Silda so Silda wrote it alone, and there's sort of a suggestion of like, free-love and bad-girl shit to come. Surfing nuns? It really goes out with a bang. Hilary is liberated from Pismo Beach and takes off with some Hells Angels.

TRIP   Silda must have been really bombed when they made that one. Listen, all anybody wants is for you to just—you know—be like, productive and *happy* and living in the world again, and they're sophisticated people, if you see some stuff differently to them, well, everybody is a grown up here, we all know how to live with that, right?

BROOKE *(a smile)*   Trip. Have you actually ever *met* our parents?

Polly comes out, sun glasses, very big ones cover her eyes.

POLLY   Okay, who's ready to go into town? I have to say, it is such a relief not to be cooking Christmas dinner this year. I can't face the idea of slaving over another eighty-pound turkey and a ham the size of a pit bull.

TRIP   Hey, mom. We were talking about the Hilary movies. Why'd you stop writing pictures? Maybe you should get back in the game.

POLLY My full-time job was your father. When he became GOP chair, it didn't seem appropriate. Also, Hollywood stopped being fun. *(beat)* At first pictures were fun, being a girl, a smart girl in the pictures. Right out of Bryn Mawr, and into the writer's building at MGM. And when your aunt and I didn't want to work together anymore, I never found anyone else to write with. But truly, once it became about drugs and lefties whining, I was out.

BROOKE Lefties whining. It always come back to that. Doesn't it? With you?

POLLY Well. *You do.* All of you! You all whine and lecture and preach.

BROOKE Yep, that's the downfall of us all, Polly, lefties whining all over the place. *(exiting)* I gotta go. I don't want to be late for my conference call with Al-Qaeda.

Trip laughs. Brooke leaves. There is silence. Polly stares at her son. He fiddles with his cell phone or something, keenly aware of being observed.

TRIP Stop staring at me. You're giving me hives.

POLLY Do you have any cigarettes hidden anywhere, Trip?

TRIP No. I am totally smoke free, Mom.

POLLY It's all or nothing with your generation. Either vegans or meth addicts or both at the same time, we have meth labs just outside of town, they blow up every now and then. The labs AND the addicts. *(beat)* How does she seem to you?

TRIP A little on edge, a little nervous, but basically you know, fine?

POLLY *(scoffs)* "Basically fine?" You have no observational skills, none at all. She's not 'a *little nervous*'; she's dancing as fast as she can, and something's up. What?

TRIP I dunno, don't ask me, Jeez. I'm not like the family goddamn spy.

POLLY   Something about her book? Did you read it? What is it, I'd really like it if someone gave me some advance warning of what to—

TRIP *(over her)*   I haven't even *looked* at it yet! Stop interrogating me, I'm not sixteen, god. She's a grown-up person, stop *studying* her like she's a specimen out of some lab.

POLLY   She's hardly a 'grown-up person', darling, she's naive, she's secretive, very, *very* private—lots of locked doors in her doll house. No, she's a little kid, honey. A smart, sly one.

TRIP   Well, you make people very nervous!

POLLY *(snapping)*   I do not make people '*very nervous*'! *(beat)* Not when they have nothing to be nervous about! But really, I worry about her. She's tanked the marriage, Cary gave up. Did you know that?

TRIP   Yeah, but she didn't 'tank' anything. That's bullshit and you know it, Polly! Cary was a class-A creep. She just liked him because he looked like Lord Byron's little faggy cousin. That sad wet Brit married her for a fucking green card, Mom. Please. He never loved her: he loved not being fucking *English*. Why don't you back your daughter instead of that mossy little prick?

POLLY   Well, A: please don't swear so much. And B: it is not out of the question that she has a trace of lesbianism in her, like my sister.

TRIP   Well, A: that would be fine. What's wrong with that? And besides—B: *(sweetly)* why are we having this talk, Polly?

POLLY   Because you're a moron.

TRIP   Yeah. So what about it?

POLLY *(emphatically)*   Because when we're gone, you're going to have to watch out for her.

TRIP   "Gone"? Where you going? You going somewhere?

POLLY   What if she has another breakdown? And we're gone? It'll be on you! You!

TRIP   She's fine. The meds.

POLLY   And when they stop working? The brain grows used to them, you know, I've read it in the *Internet!*

TRIP   You read it *in* the Internet? Oh well, then it *must* be true! Why are you *saying* this? She is *fine!* She just finished writing a book! She sold it! She's back on her feet! God, you never worried about me like that.

POLLY *(snapping)*   Because I didn't have to! Life for you has always been easy, despite the horrific habit you have of putting question marks at the end of so many sentences unnecessarily.

TRIP *(grinning)*   Thanks?

POLLY   It runs in the family. The despair. Your brother. He couldn't outrun it. It made him crazy. It runs in the family, on Lyman's side, Scots blood, not mine, very cheerful people from my side, Texans, Westerners.

TRIP   You mean rabbis, don't you?

POLLY   Families get terrorized by their weakest member, it's true. Look at me; I've had to take care of Silda ALL my life. She doesn't have a cent, she is alive thanks to us, and she has to live within spitting distance. Please. Now she has to live HERE. Until I get your dad to buy that house next door and stock it with Philipino nurses I can't even go to Europe for fear of her having some sort of catastrophe—whenever we go anywhere she does something absurd like cut her hand off in a mixmaster or something. *(beat)*

TRIP   She cut off her *hand?*

POLLY *(smiling)*   You know what I mean. *God.* She was making a mojito and the blade slipped.

The two of them try not to laugh, but really, they can't help it.

POLLY *(cont.)* She needed about two thousand stitches. *(beat)* And I always am propping up your father too! Your sister worries him so badly! He just stares out into the desert and frets.

A pause, and Trip decides to go for it. He is simple and clear.

TRIP Okay, well, Mom, since we're being serious here: you know what I think? You're unbelievably rough on her. You can't handle it when people hit bumps—it totally freaks you out—you want everyone to be a goddamn marine, okay, Polly?

POLLY Yes, I don't like weakness. I've tried to push her, to be hard on her so that she wouldn't sink. I don't know if I've succeeded. You can die from too much sensitivity in this world.

TRIP *(a smile)* Yeah, well. That's sure not gonna happen to you.

POLLY She has no idea what it means to roll with the punches, to let it ride.

TRIP Yeah? Like you do?

POLLY *Please* take me seriously.

TRIP Right. Okay. I will.

POLLY I *dread* reading this thing. It's so much pressure. So much pressure to be fair. I *hate* being fair.

TRIP *(a laugh)* They should put that on your tombstone. "Here lies Polly Wyeth. She hated being fair." *(Beat. He kisses her.)* But you are, Mom.

POLLY I'm just telling you that your sister will be *your* problem one day, Trip. Okay?

TRIP She won't be. Nobody's anybody's goddamn problem!

SILDA GRAUMAN *enters. A mess. No makeup, hair disheveled. She wears a muumuu, and carries a pill case marked with the days of the week, and takes some as she talks. Trip gets her a glass of water.*

SILDA *(making an entrance)*   Hey kids! Oh boy! Wooh. Jesus Christ, you know what happens when you don't drink? *You have dreams.*

Polly and Trip stand smiling at her.

SILDA *(cont.)*   I hate dreams. I have more Nazi dreams than Elie Wiesel! What does that say about me, always being chased by the S.S.? *(she takes in Trip)* Hello, Trip sweetie, you look like a million bucks, so cute! *(beat)* Maybe it's the pills they have me on. They gave me this antabuse stuff. You know what it is? If you drink you can't stop throwing up, believe me, I've weighed the options. Jesus, what day is it? I'm taking Tuesday for Thursday. I mean, what kinda doctor *invents* something like that? Huh? Some goddamn avaricious sadist in the pocket of the drug companies, is who. *Where's my niece?*

POLLY   Hello, Silda. Did you sleep well?

SILDA *(scoffs)*   Sleep *well?* How do you sleep well on that farkakte tempurpedic? This *not drinking* is gonna kill me—remember that great Totie Fields joke: *"I've been on a diet for fourteen days and all I've lost is two weeks"*? That's how I feel about not drinking. Of course, she got so fat I'll bet she didn't think it was funny when they lopped her leg off from the diabetes. I guess there's a cautionary tale in there, isn't there? *Oh fuck!* I forgot it's Christmas Eve today, isn't it? Trip, I hope you don't mind, I didn't get presents, I can't—I'm not allowed to drive anymore, and—

TRIP	**SILDA** *(a laugh, a bark)*
No, no presents—	And I'm broke, of course, so there's that—

SILDA *(cont.)*   Well, thank Christ I can still swim. I'm gonna jump in the pool and try and do a couple laps before the end of the day here.

She exits. A dervish leaving them slightly undone in her wake.

Polly looks at her son.

POLLY And there you have it, a preview of coming attractions for you, Trip. *And that's* as good as it gets, my dear. That's as good as it gets.

Blackout

SCENE TWO

The Wyeth living room, late afternoon. Christmas Eve. The sun is going down, an ochre desert light pervades. The Christmas tree is lit, in all it's splendor. Silda and Polly are wrapping a few last presents. Silda wears a Pucci-like top. The fire is lit. Silda is smoking Virginia Slims. Polly is drinking a scotch, rocks.

SILDA Yeah, yeah, yeah, I know I shouldn't smoke, but all these goddamn virtues will just kill us all, really.

POLLY Oh, I know you think that, sis.

SILDA Don't be so smug. Helen Bloom quit a year ago and then got mowed down by a garbage truck on Bob Hope Drive and she could a had a hell of a last year. Smoking like a chimney, not being tense, all of it. It was her biggest pleasure and she quit for nothing. A lost year of happiness.

POLLY Silda. Is this your way of saying you want to keep on drinking? Is that what this is?

SILDA *(a shrug)* Honey—If I wanted to, I would. I don't. So I won't.

POLLY Helen Bloom died? I thought she just dropped us.

SILDA She did drop you. And then she died.

POLLY Maybe they're connected. Why did she drop us?

SILDA Why does anyone drop you? Because you're not an easy person. I'd drop you too if I could. *(beat)* Do you like the Pucci I'm wearing?

POLLY Do you mean—do I like the quote/unquote "Pucci" you're wearing?

SILDA   Please don't start with me! There was a sale. I had to fight off three old vultures for this Pucci! It was like something from *National Geographic.*

POLLY   This Pucci was made in a basement in Rangoon, please! All these phony designer dresses and tacky Hong Kong knock-offs you scrounge for at Loehmann's; they never fool anybody, really.

SILDA   This Pucci is quite, quite real!

The gift wrapping ceases.

POLLY   Darling. I know when I'm being played. I know what's real and what isn't.

SILDA   *(dead serious)*   They don't have fake at Loehmann's!

POLLY   Right. They have originals for fourteen ninety-five. It's a miracle!

SILDA   *(getting angry)*   Polly! Stop that! That's mean. What's the matter with you?

POLLY   I'll tell you what's wrong: the buttons are wrong! The colors are off! Listen—there's no shame in being careful, in having to scrounge for bargains, it's admirable! It's the trying to pass that gets me! *(beat)* All I am saying is, don't try and pull one over on me, I don't like it when people pretend things are one thing and they're actually clearly another.

My daughter is tap dancing around about this book of hers and we're sitting here *waiting* like nothing is happening. I mean, I could take it out of her goddman bag. If I were to sneak it, which is something *you* would do, that would put me on the defensive, because the discussion would become about *that,* rather than the thing itself! So no, we can play that game. Oh, I can wait, but let's not pretend that those are real buttons.

Silda stares at her sister, nodding. She then starts to laugh.

SILDA   You know, I am going to have to learn how to deal with you now that I'm sober. Because if I were drinking, that train of thought would make sense to me, but sober, what you just said is totally incomprehensible.

POLLY   Before she died, Helen Bloom quit my book club, you know.

SILDA   *I know all about it.* But that wasn't a *book club*; it was a vast right-wing conspiracy! See, your politics are offensive to normal people. You goad people with them.

POLLY   I like to spar.

SILDA   That's what Atilla the Hun said! That's why you two are so isolated here! Your only social life is with that blue-hair republican crowd. All those fund-raisers you do or go to, all those hopeless squares. You used to be so with-it! When we were kids.

Polly sighs, gets up, pours herself another drink.

POLLY   Silda. I love those fund-raisers. I believe in them. I believe in that 'crowd'. They're my people. They have a stake in upholding the entrepreneurial American spirit. I'm still a Texas girl, Silda. So are you.

SILDA *(looking at her)*   Honey. News-flash: you're not a Texan, you're a Jew! We're Jewish girls who lost their accents along the way, but for you that wasn't enough, you had to become a goy, too. Talk about the real thing? Talk about 'faking it'. Honey, this Pucci is a lot more real than your Pat Buckley schtick.

POLLY   Try not to be disagreeable, Silda, it's Christmas.

Lyman enters, he's dressed for dinner; country club casual elegance from slightly another time.

LYMAN *(kissing them both)*   Hello, my darlings. The two most beautiful women of the desert!

SILDA *(happy to see him)*   Hey, Lyman, *Submarine Captain* was on the Turner channel last night. They're doing a Christmas of war pictures from the old days.

LYMAN   A Christmas of *war pictures*?

SILDA   What can I say? It cheers people up. This is America, we get warm and fuzzy about war. It took you about twelve minutes to die, not including commercials.

LYMAN *(a small smile)*   It's true. Nobody at Warner's died like me. It's the one thing I had a knack for. *(He demonstrates dying in a fusillade of gunfire, to the delight of his two girls.) (beat)* Before the kids get back, I want to ask that we give Brooke some breathing room this evening. Palm Springs should be a refuge, where she wants to come to when life in New York gets unbearable for her.

SILDA   Palm Springs isn't a refuge; it's King Tut's tomb. The whole town is filled with mummies with tans.

LYMAN   I don't want confrontations. First time she's been here in six years, and I want her to want to come back. Often. And easily. To feel safe here.

POLLY *(a sigh)*   Lyman thinks I am too stark with her.

LYMAN *(smiling, but pointed)*   Actually, Lyman thinks his wife doesn't take well to constructive criticism, is what Lyman thinks. Okay?

He kisses her. She rebuffs him playfully.

POLLY   I just think—The only way to get someone to not be an invalid is to refuse to treat them as such.

SILDA   And there it is, folks: the entire GOP platform in a nutshell.

POLLY   If I were to be gentle with you, you'd never get out of bed.

Brooke and Trip enter, laden with shopping bags, Christmas presents.

TRIP   Hola and stuff.

SILDA   Oh good, you're back!

BROOKE *(cheerful, maybe somewhat manic)*   My GOD! It's insane out there. The Christmas decorations—a papier-mâché reindeer and a menorah fell onto Palm Canyon Drive and traffic is backed up for miles—the lights sparked a fire, and the reindeer burnt up like an effigy of George Bush in Baghdad! I forget *how hallucinatory*, it can be here on the West Coast.

SILDA   I gotta get out of this place.

BROOKE   You can always move east with me. I have room.

SILDA   *(a scoff)*   Yeah, me in the snow, that'll work.

TRIP   Hey, why have we *never* gone to that Desert Follies thing? Do you *realize* the world's *oldest living show girl* is performing *nightly*?

SILDA   *(a shrug; they're pals)*   Sure—Dorothy Dale.

TRIP   I wanna—the best Christmas present you could give me, is we go downtown, have funny drinks and watch the hoofers. Please? I mean, she's in the *Guinness Book of World Records*!

POLLY   I think we may have just found the next foreman for *Jury of Your Peers*.

Brooke puts down her shopping bags. She takes out two boxes, the kind you get from a copy store for manuscripts.

BROOKE   Okay, here. Two copies. Freshly printed. I know you've been waiting. Just let's get this over with and go on to enjoy ourselves.

And silence. What to make of her?

TRIP   *(flat)*   Merry Christmas. Santa has come early. Yay!

The family stares at Brooke.

BROOKE   *(brightly)*   Come on! I don't want there to be any more anxious stares. No more fear, no more dread . . .

Brooke pours herself a drink. Lyman looks at Trip, who shrugs, "I dunno."

LYMAN   "Dread"!   *(slowly)*   Should we be dreading this novel, darling?

BROOKE   No. No, no, no no, no. Sorry! Wrong word. Not dread, but there *is* something you should know before you read it.

POLLY Oh, I love it when people say there's something you should know—you can just tell it's something you wish you didn't have to hear.

LYMAN Stop it Polly.

BROOKE *(quietly)* Well first off, it's not a novel. I know I said it was and it started off as one. But after a few chapters, there was no hiding what it was, no fighting it. It's a *memoir*.

LYMAN A memoir? Of . . . ?

BROOKE Us. The story of everything that happened to us. So I wanted to prepare you for this.

POLLY Ah, I see. So you want us to brace ourselves. And that's why you've been hesitant to tell us earlier. You thought we couldn't handle it?

BROOKE I had to finish writing it to make sure, and to know what I had. To sit with it.

LYMAN *(carefully)* Well, it's not entirely unexpected. May I ask what's in it?

POLLY Actually probably the more piquant question is—what's not, isn't it, Brooke?

BROOKE Look. *(open, clear)* Here's what it is: I was blocked. As the entire *world* knows. And then something clicked. After you sent me all my old diaries, Dad, you know, all those boxes. Something was triggered. About the life we had. The thing of you being old guard Republicans in Hollywood, that odd and very particular subset. What it was like to be the child of an ambassador. And how that affected us, all of us—how it made us.

POLLY In other words, it's all about your *brother*, of course.

BROOKE Yes. It's mostly Henry. And yes. Yes. Your relationship with him. *(beat)* What happened to that boy, who loved music, who made me sit between two speakers and memorize all the lyrics to every Beach Boys song?

Beat

POLLY *(looks at Brooke)*   Brooke. I just want to say this: You may of course write whatever you like, but the ice gets thin, the ice gets thin when it involves WE the living. We, the living, would like to go out gracefully.

TRIP *(impatient)*   Hey, hey—I have an idea, why don't we all *read* it before someone, like, says some *shit* they might want to retract later or something. You're all asking questions—they can all be— let's just have Christmas first please. I mean, can't we try really hard to muster up some normalcy, for *me,* as like, a Christmas present. Okay? Huh?

Beat

LYMAN *(deciding)*   Well, I don't need to read it. I can give you my stamp, say what you will. I am at peace.

POLLY *(astonished)*   Peace? Lyman! No, you're not.

LYMAN *(clearly)*   Polly. No. Sorry. I bow out. Quite simply, I do not wish to adjudicate what our daughter has written.

BROOKE   You don't want to look at it?

LYMAN   I will not be put in the position of—

POLLY   "Decider"? Well, I will. You and I have a son. Who was implicated in a horrific and senseless *bombing.* In which a homeless veteran of Vietnam was burnt to death. Burnt to a crisp. Supposedly by accident. *And that* is the subject of her book! So, no, I am not at "peace".

LYMAN *(a kind of quiet command, not to be contradicted)*   Polly. Let it be. That's not how I conduct myself. I never have. It doesn't work.

BROOKE   Look, I love you. And *nothing* in it contradicts that. Really, I don't think you have anything to be nervous about.

POLLY Said the spider to the fly?

BROOKE *(a bitter laugh)* I just love how—right off the bat, you assume that it's a hit-and-run job on you, Mom. How little trust there is. Look at you.

POLLY "Trust"! Didn't Ronnie say 'trust but *verify*'? I kind of would like to verify! Before it shows up on the bedside tables of the liberal elite across the land? Before we're reviewed by your pal, Ms. Didion, in *The New York Review of Books*.

BROOKE Wow.

LYMAN *(another gentleman's smile)* Let's not rush to any conclusions, shall we? If you got a decent advance, we could always give it back. If that's an issue.

BROOKE No. Jesus. *(laughing)* Knopf bought it. I'd probably make more money selling cashews in Central Park, but it's something, and it buys me time to do another. This is good! Really, I mean—

POLLY That is not in dispute, of course it's good. You're a real writer, you shouldn't have been fulminating in the dark for seven years.

BROOKE *(blowing up)* Jesus Christ, '*fulminating*'? Is that what you call being hospitalized? Is that what you call what was going on with me?

POLLY No. I don't. I know what was going on with you.

Polly looks strained. She glances at Lyman. Silda lights a smoke.

SILDA Polly, you're being really, and I mean *really*, a hard-ass, even by your standards, which is saying a lot. She's written a new book, she's sold it, she's had tough times, tougher than you understand and—

POLLY *(over her)* Oh, I *understand*, I was there. I fed her when she refused to eat. I sat there in Sag Harbor in that dark little cottage— *don't you dare* tell me I don't understand my daughter! That is one area, the area of having children, where you can not presume to condescend to me, because when I am called, *I* show up, okay?

In the wake of that, there is silence. Trip sighs, shakes his head and sits down.

TRIP   And so much for yuletide cheer.

Beat

POLLY   A friend of mine's stepson wrote a book, a lovely San Francisco family; all about his shitty childhood and his boarding school horrors, booze and acne, now there are lawsuits for everyone. And it was in all the papers, she had to move to Andorra, Spain, or some crazy goddamn place and hide amongst the Basques. Of course, the book made the little shit's reputation and now he's living it up, you probably *know* him, you all probably go have tapas together in the fucking Village, right?

BROOKE   Is this acting, is this schtick? I can't tell if you're putting on an act or if this is real.

POLLY   "*Acting or real*"? The two are hardly mutually exclusive in this family.

LYMAN   Stop, please. Please. You're both giving me a headache. Truce. Okay? Peace.

There is a moment of truce.

LYMAN *(cont.)*   Forget the goddamn book. We can take our time. Right? It takes a while to put out a book. SO we can—why don't we not even look at it until after the holidays? After the New Year. And just enjoy this time together. *(slightly furious)* This discussion can wait. And it will. Is that clear?

There is silence. Lyman knows how to stop a room; he's played lawyers and been an ambassador, so even though its performance, it still is jarring, given his gentleness.

BROOKE   Yes. It does take a while to publish a book. Next fall, in fact. Almost a year.

LYMAN *(he's won)*   So WHY are we doing this? There's time. Good, so let's bank our fires. We really don't have to do this now at all.

BROOKE   Well.

There is a long silence. Lyman looks around. "What?"

BROOKE *(cont.)*   The New Yorker.

LYMAN   Yes?

BROOKE   Something fell out and there was a slot and my editor gave it to them, and they're going to run it in February.

LYMAN   I see. Two months away. Ahhh. I see.

BROOKE   They close the issue a bit ahead so there isn't so much time. They have a deadline and it's right before the first of the year, you see, if there's anything you really need to have your say about, it's got to be soon.

There is a stunned silence. Polly lets out a laugh of disbelief.

POLLY   *The New Yorker* is publishing sections of a book about us?

BROOKE   Yes.

POLLY *(shaking her head, wry as hell)*   And a Happy New Year. *(to Lyman)* Two seats for Andorra please.

BROOKE *(looks at Trip)*   Sorry.

TRIP *(surprised, annoyed)*   Pretty selective in what we share, aren't we, Brooke? Jesus.

LYMAN *(somewhat hardened)*   I don't know that I entirely like the way this is happening. I don't see why this has to be hurriedly—I appreciate that you're asking us for our blessing, and giving us the opportunity, as scant as it is, to weigh in here but . . .

BROOKE *(quietly)*   I don't understand what there is to be afraid of. I am not allowed to—am I not—is there a blanket ban on writing about my life if it involves anyone else?

POLLY   I could sue you, but that would make an even bigger splash.

BROOKE *(bursts into laughter)*   You could *sue* me?

POLLY *(good natured)*   Sure. Families do it all the time. Ask Trip! Half the goddamn people on his show are families suing each other over unpaid parking tickets and negligent fratricide or something! Why shouldn't we get in on the act? Maybe we could do it on Trip's show! We could be part of the freaks!

TRIP   Ours is small claims, you'd need the war crimes tribunal in the Hague, mom.

Polly laughs, she likes it.

POLLY   Trip. Let me ask you something: A girl shows up on your TV show, having exploited for profit a personal tragedy without consulting the people who were also affected by it; what would your jury of peers say to that? Would they approve? Or would they say 'stone her'?

LYMAN   Jesus, please.

BROOKE   *"Stone her."* That's great.

TRIP   You know what? All of you—there are at least three places I could have been right now: Cape Town, Punte del Este, or Bahia. There are girls with fun families in beach-houses where you can swim and drink and laugh and nobody is trying to fucking, you know, assassinate each other over a goddamn book. *(beat)* Over a BOOK! That is of almost zero-point-one conceivable percent interest to ANYONE I know! And I know a lot of people. I have learned so much about families from my show. *(he laughs)* The way in which the bored and the damaged ruin whatever little bit of happiness they happen to have. And I always want to tell them 'hey, you schmucks, you have wasted one more day of living better'.

There is silence.

TRIP *(cont.)*   But me? I'm pretty goddamn happy, and I'm not going to let you all take that away from me. *(beat)* I have reservations on three flights to distant cities for tomorrow and I will only be cancelling two of them at this rate. *(He looks at his mother)* So as to "would I stone her?". See, I'm not asking for peace like Dad is. Mom, I'm just telling you, I love everyone here, and I won't be played. Not by any one of you.

BROOKE I'm so sorry, Trip. I don't mean for you to be in the middle of it. This. Mess.

TRIP Yeah, well. (*beat*) You're a really good writer, Brooke. Seriously. But you ...

He stops, shakes his head. He walks out. Brooke sits down, nodding. Silence.

LYMAN (*to Silda, gently*) Silda, I wonder if you would make me some tea? Would you mind, please?

SILDA Of course, sweetie. Two sugars? Milk?

LYMAN Lemon. Honey.

SILDA Anybody else?

BROOKE Please. Thank you.

After she gives Brooke a quick look of solidarity, perhaps even a gesture, Silda exits to the kitchen.

BROOKE (*cont.*) Okay. So.

POLLY Why is it that children are allowed a sort of endless series of free passes in this life, you know, and we're expected to be the parents of children forever? This is a new phenomenon; once I was an adult, all of my parents' indulgence ceased. You all want to stay children forever, doing whatever mischief you can think of. All you entitled children of the "me" generation.

BROOKE (*delighted*) By free-passes you mean "free-will" of course? And I don't particularly remember feeling indulged, but that's just a matter of point of view I suppose; but let's really clarify something—I am not looking for a free-pass from you, or any sort of pass at all.

POLLY (*emphatic*) Then what do you want? Tell me exactly what you want!

Brooke stands there. Tortured and considering the question.

BROOKE   I don't know. I don't *know* if I can go ahead with it without your blessing. But I might have to try and do just that.

POLLY   Honey, you want our blessing? If this book is what I think it is, you're gonna get a lot of attention, and you're going to have to be able to handle it, and if you get flustered with me, how are you going to handle the public, strangers?

BROOKE *(laughing)*   How? Strangers are a cake walk compared to you, Polly.

POLLY   I knew before you got here that this is where it was going. I could tell because you're my daughter and everything else you ever wrote you sent us before the ink was dry on the paper!

BROOKE   Well, you certainly always took your time responding! What's the goddamn rush NOW? All of a sudden, huh?

LYMAN *(finally pissed off)*   Oh, Jesus, both of you stop it, this is absurd.

POLLY   The story of your brother. It's drugs. Your whole generation, awash in drugs. The provocations, the absurd beard, the refusal to shower, to bathe, to adhere to the basic civilities of family life. He was stoned from the age of fifteen on, it made him dumb and it triggered his depression. Three generations, three generations of escapism. Lost. Drugs. Drugs actually destroyed the American century. Up the hill there, up the hill in Indio, the meth addicts, and you see them coming into town, wrecks.

She lights up. Thinks.

POLLY *(cont.)*   I can quite honestly say I dread this. Really, really, dread this.

BROOKE   I'm sorry. I can not write again about ephemera, about Paul Bowles' haunts in Tangier for *Travel & Leisure,* I can't interview one more Iranian filmmaker, and I can't try to dissect

Salt Lake City for Manhattanites. It's all I've got you see. *(suddenly furious)* I don't have an imagination! WE are all I have.

POLLY   You used to believe in yourself! How did you learn to think so little of your powers? Your novel, your first book, it's beautiful, exquisitely observed.

BROOKE *(gently, over her)*   Thank you, but I don't *want* to talk about my powers, I want to talk about Henry until it makes sense. The silence where he once was. His part in something terrible. *(a growing anger)* How when he came to you for help, you didn't. You sent him away. He was your son. No matter what he did. He was your son!

POLLY *(not to be overrun by her daughter)*   Okay then! Okay! Okay, then so, *that's your take.*

BROOKE   Yes it is. *(beat, hardened)* I imagine his suicide. His last day. I try to understand the note he left. I do that, that's in there, too.

LYMAN   You imagine his suicide.

BROOKE   To try and make sense of it. What that day was like for him. Drowning.

LYMAN *(bewildered)*   Why?

BROOKE   Because I think I died too.

LYMAN *(imploring)*   But you didn't, darling. Look at you. You're right here. You have a life. You struggled. Yes, I know you were scarred but all things considered, haven't you prevailed?

BROOKE   *This* is prevailing? *(beat)* My brother killed himself. He was my best friend and he didn't even leave me a note. Why did he leave *you* a note, and not me? That doesn't make any sense. To jump off a ferry in freezing water? Never found. You don't leave people that way. It's stealing their life as well.

Brooke stops, composes herself. Polly looks stricken, tortured, briefly, seeing her daughter in such evident pain. Lyman takes in the scene; it is slipping out of his hands.

35

LYMAN *(quietly)* We shouldn't be doing this. We haven't even read it.

POLLY That is true. *(getting up)* Well. I'm gonna go do me some light reading, kids.

Polly crosses to Brooke.

POLLY *(cont.)* Whatever it is, whatever you do, you're our daughter, and I will love you. I can't stop you from doing what you will, I can't prevent it. But you must know that whatever you do, there are consequences to your actions.

BROOKE What does that mean?

POLLY How could I trust you? How could I ever be in your presence, my dear? If you betrayed the trust of the family? A family that has so valued discretion and our good name in the past three decades. You would still be my daughter, but the meaning of it would change. You needed us. We came to the East Coast. A year of our lives, I thought of nothing but your well-being, your recovery. I could never in quite the same way avail myself—I know who I am. That is who I am. You would lose us. So you understand.

Polly kisses Brooke, exits to the bedroom. Lyman stands there, smiling, tense. Lyman goes over to the Scandinavian fireplace.

BROOKE *(a laugh)* Wow. *That* was a scary kiss. Is that right, Dad? I would lose you?

Lyman looks at the suspended fireplace, shakes his head.

LYMAN Never ceases to surprise me how cold it gets out here in the desert at night.

He puts some logs in the fire. The glow is intense.

LYMAN *(cont.)* So, is this going how you expected?

BROOKE *(helpless)* I thought, as in all things, you would give me your blanket support, cheer me on. "What did I expect"? I don't work that way, I follow my stupid impulses to the bitter end.

LYMAN *(quiet, but direct)* You could postpone the magazine piece. So I could slowly persuade your mother that it doesn't matter.

Brooke looks at her dad. And then he is negotiating, seamless.

LYMAN *(cont.)* Brooke. I am looking for room to navigate, for this to feel less like we are cornered. You have to give people room to navigate, you must leave people options.

BROOKE Politics has given you the idea that all things are negotiable, Lyman. It's why people can't bear politics anymore. Everything is forever on the table.

LYMAN *(frustrated)* This has nothing to do with politics. *I'm frightened.* In two months, the most painful part of our lives will be in the glossy pages of a magazine, and then a few months later, a *book.*

She goes to him and hugs him, a daughter's sudden impulse, to ameliorate this. He doesn't know what to do, and slowly pulls away, torn.

LYMAN *(cont.)* I'm going to go outside for a bit. I need to smoke. Get some more firewood.

Lyman exits. Brooke is alone onstage. Lost in a kind of dread. Silda enters. Bearing tea on a tray.

SILDA So . . . ?

She gives her niece a cup.

BROOKE I miscalculated. Badly. Polly basically threatened to never speak to me again.

SILDA Really? I'd take that deal in a goddamn heartbeat, kid.

BROOKE *(can't help but laugh)* Did you know, Silda? When I kept sending you pages—did you know that this was how they'd react?

SILDA Of course I did. You're surprised?

BROOKE I'm always surprised.

SILDA What? You thought there would be no consequences to telling the truth? Telling the truth is a very expensive hobby. At least yours leaves you with something. My little hobbies left me broke.

BROOKE I could hold off. I mean, I finished it. Maybe that's enough for now—just knowing it was done—without needing it out in the world for a bit—

SILDA *(appalled, cuts her off)* Don't you dare!

BROOKE It's not that I'm scared, it's just that I don't want to be unkind—

SILDA *(sharp and bitter)* To these terribly kind people?

BROOKE My father, Silda, is not unkind. That's the part I just can't . . .

She stops, shakes her head. She looks stricken. Silda nods. Giving her niece that.

SILDA I wish you'd let me give you some concealer, you have those dark circles under your eyes. You just need some *TV Touch,* honey.

BROOKE *(bursts out laughing)* You and your TV Touch. Jesus, you think that's what I need? A goddamn *makeover?*

Silda delves into her purse and comes out with a little pot of makeup, which Brooke submits to.

SILDA Hold still, you're so jumpy. What? You want a Xanax or something? I have a whole goddamn Halloween bag of the stuff.

BROOKE *(exhausted but smiling)* Please—I beg you. Stop trying to make me laugh—this is not in the slightest bit funny.

SILDA *(quietly, while applying makeup)* Okay. No. Lyman is not unkind. But. *(beat)* But life is chemical. And a chemical reaction happens when two people get together, and in this case, a certain kind of ambition, and striving overtook the actual human beings. Your parents are holding onto the last bits of power and influence they had, and they can't imagine a world in which you have the right to speak of it. Critically. *(beat)* They tried so hard to turn Henry into one of them; cut his hair, sent him to a boarding school for delinquents, forbid him to express any antiwar sentiment in their home, forbid his friends to enter the house—they tried to clean him up, but he fought as hard as he could. I tried to protect him— to give him something. But I was no match. *(beat)* These people, driven by fear, have taken ownership of an entire country. And fear—fear led to punishment and in the case of your brother, even at the cost of a life itself—just to hold on to the 'way things were'. You managed to explain in one little book, *in one book.* And you did it just by telling the story of this family. *(beat)* Isn't that something?

Silda stares at Brooke, not doing her makeup for a moment. When she goes on, it is with great clarity, specificity, urgency.

SILDA *(cont.)*   So, please. I am begging you. Don't back down. Brooke: you are stronger than Henry was. Your book gives him everything I couldn't. And I am telling you what I told him! "Do what you must! Fight on." *(beat)* Don't back down. Do it for him, for Henry, do not back down! You'll win, because you have ideas, and they only have fear!

BROOKE *(looking around the room)*   There are no pictures of him. How do you do that? Have no pictures of your son? Look around: Sinatra, Rock Hudson, you, Barry Goldwater, me, me and Trip in Mexico, Nancy, Dad in any number of movies. Look at him. Mom and Dinah Shore.

SILDA   I introduced them. They had chemistry.

BROOKE *(she picks up a picture)*   One picture of Henry. Age seventeen. In Ojai at school. Look. He looked like the best of both of them. He was supposed to be an actor. He played Hamlet in high school. He understood that play. All that ambivalence. All that rage, God, he understood it. Tall, long shock of hair, silent, quiet, royal. But this surfer version, this California golden boy Hamlet.

Lyman has returned with an armful of firewood. He drops it next to the fireplace.

LYMAN *(quiet, dark)*   He was wonderful. He would have been a movie star.

SILDA   Your tea.

She points to the cup and saucer. Lyman nods.

SILDA *(cont.)*   Are you okay?

LYMAN *(something distant about him, keeping his own counsel)*   I think I might be catching a bit of something. A little bug of some sort.

Silda goes to the bar and pours whiskey into his cup.

SILDA   This'll help. God knows.

He takes a sip.

LYMAN *(beat, quietly)*   I never wrote my memoir, because it would have hurt our friends, how hard it was, after Henry was implicated the way he was, how they all vanished and your mother refused to accept it. She circled the wagons. Around me. Borne out of thinking I'm easily bruised. I am not easily bruised. *(Beat. There is a certain intense, lost quality in his telling of this. It is not easy; a story never shared. It is an illustrative story, meant to draw her in.)* But she would not let them off the hook, she's the only woman to have faced down Nancy Reagan, Betsy Bloomingdale, and Mrs. Annenberg at the same lunch and reduced them all to tears. Tears of shame for their unconscionable behavior—*(a growl)*. As though *I* had placed that bomb. Your mother reminded them all who we really were, and of their obligations to honor loyal friends— Nancy went to Ronnie and sat him down, they had a dinner for us at the L.A. Country Club and everyone came out. Yes. Now they were our friends again. And by the time Ronnie was president, they made me ambassador . . .

His eyes well up, he grins through it, the way older men do, when telling these sorts of stories.

BROOKE I didn't know it went down like that. That mom did that.

LYMAN *(imploring)* Please don't do this. *I can not* embarrass those people. They're, some of them, alive still—! You can do what you like after we're gone! Do you not understand that? It's simply good manners. It's as simple as that!

BROOKE *(serious and quiet)* Well, let me tell you, good manners have got me into a lot of trouble, Dad. Probably you too. I am past the point of good manners.

LYMAN *(and finally, knowing he lost, letting the bitterness come out, unmasked, no longer the diplomat)* You have so much of your mother in you. You don't like any weakness, especially in yourself. You can't forgive it. *(beat)* It is why you ended up in a damn hospital! Well—if you can't forgive yourself, I suppose it's futile to ask that you to forgive me! No. *(his voice rises)* So you'll publish your book and punish us all, and a reporter will call me for a comment! *(his voice choking)* And I will say "no comment." *(furious)* I will keep saying it until I die! "No comment"!

Lyman exits. Silence. Brooke is shaken.

She has not seen this Lyman, this side of him, directed at her.

Silda finally picks up Lyman's empty tea cup, and deeply smells the residual booze in it. She breathes deeply.

SILDA God, I love that smell, that vapor, if I could just live in that scent, I'd be happy. I'd never need to take a drink again, I'd just breathe it in.

Blackout
End of Act One

ACT II

Some hours have passed.

It is night.

The fireplace glowing. Silda is asleep on the sofa, a throw covering her. Brooke and Trip alone in the living room. They are drinking whiskey. Trip is reading the manuscript, and Brooke is pacing, anxious, making herself known.

TRIP *(finally, exasperated with her, stops reading)*   I could make us a sandwich. You haven't eaten since breakfast.

BROOKE *(brightly)*   Oh god. Not really very hungry, actually.

TRIP   You're not supposed to *not* eat, Brooke. *(beat, a sigh)* I was looking forward to all that strange food at the country club. Crab legs. A whole roast pig. And then there's suddenly like Pad Thai and rellenos. Crazy mix.

BROOKE   I think I have successfully demolished Christmas Eve. *(looking toward her parents' bedroom)* They've been in there far too long.

TRIP *(smiling)*   Preparing the attack.

BROOKE *(a tense smile in return)*   How can you stay so neutral on this?

TRIP   Who said I was neutral? I just said I'm still absorbing it all.

BROOKE   So you support me?

TRIP   I didn't say that, did I? Look, I haven't read the whole thing from start to finish, but enough. You (probably) have the right to publish anything you like, pretty much about anyone, whether it's decent or cool or not, and they have the right to push back whether *that's* decent or cool or not.

BROOKE You're like Mom. It's like you learned chess in her womb and are playing against yourself and everyone else is only a pawn.

TRIP *(he stares at her, amazed)* What do you want? For me to say 'Oh boy sis—*sure*—"art" comes before life'?

BROOKE No. That's the worst kind of oversimplification.

TRIP *(grinning)* But you sort of think it *does*. And so, you have to accept the consequences of 'art over life', which in this case is likely to be losing the trust of the people you love, for the sake of these *opinions,* these bewildering *portraits* of these people who seem totally unrecognizable to me.

BROOKE Well, maybe your powers of observation . . .

TRIP *(over her)* Let me finish, since you wanna know. *(beat)* Opinions: you turn Henry into a saint of the seventies, all patchouli and innocent questioning and reacting to the stultifying oppressiveness of these Waspified GOP zombies in the other room—and it just seems to me that maybe he was really, really sick and fucked up and needed a lot of help, and was hanging out with mad bombers at very least. I mean, Christ, I was five when this happened and reading it made ME feel guilty. But Mom and Dad: you think they don't blame themselves?

BROOKE They let him go. They weren't helping him, they kicked him out—

TRIP But—did they let him go? Or did he just fly off in rage and fury. It seems you're looking for an apology, well, maybe they have apologized and you just haven't noticed it. *(the last is said very emphatically)*

BROOKE An apology? You don't write a book because you want apologies, Trip, you write a book because of who you are—a person who writes books—the only obligation I have is to myself.

To write it. Well, that's as far as it goes. I am not a publicist, I am not a hagiographer, I am a writer and this is my flawed version of what happened. I did not come here to be emotionally blackmailed and censored by two people who lived very public lives and then hid in the desert.

TRIP *(smiling, maybe, but not friendly)*   A: don't really need the lecture on what a writer is, and B: it's just a story! A story you have told yourself and will now share for fame and money and—

BROOKE   Please don't say I'm doing this for money, okay—I have no interest in money, you know that.

TRIP *(laughing)*   Yeah! Because you're *rich*. Even if you don't take a cent from them, which is not strictly true, because they paid for the fancy hospital in Cambridge where you camped out for six months—

BROOKE	**TRIP**
I wasn't camping—	You're rich, you're smart, absurdly white, Ivy League, New York, and your parents are rich and you know it—

BROOKE   And what about you? What are you, a Zapotec Indian?

TRIP *(simple)*   The difference between *us* is, I don't use my sixteen dozen different little sickness for gain. *(beat)* You do. It's just who you are. You think being a depressive makes you special? Guess what, being depressed makes you banal. And in your case, hard. Not easy to be with.

BROOKE   That's not fair.

TRIP   Fair? Well. Neither is "*Love & Mercy: A Memoir*". And I worship you, I totally do, I *love* you. But this is true. What I am about to say. Suck it up and take it. And don't interrupt. *(serious)* Because you had a breakdown, you actually believe you have earned a free-pass here. Because you couldn't function, you didn't care to eat or brush your teeth or wash your hair or even pretty much speak, and even at a point looked like you might follow Henry down the trail to off yourself—you think this entitles you to present a picture to the world of two people who failed in every possible context, as citizens, as parents, as humans.

BROOKE *(choked, tight)* You figured all this out, did you? Dr. Wyeth? When you weren't busy cooking up *Jury of Your Goddamn Peers*?

TRIP *(a smile)* You wanna be a little bitch about my TV show, Brooke? At least, at the very least, have the decency to watch it first, okay? You think you're not like anyone else on *Oprah*?

BROOKE Don't talk to me like Mom talks to Silda.

TRIP *(very sharp)* Mom talks to Silda like she loves her. And—as for my being like Mom—listen, you're as hard as fucking Stalin, and as good at chess as anyone I've ever known, and you didn't get that from Lyman.

BROOKE Look, I accept that you can't recognize our parents as I have written them, that time changed them, so why can't you accept that I've been as honest as I could in depicting events that you weren't really aware of as a little kid?

TRIP *(overlap)* I never said you were being dishonest. Let me ask you a question: Did you give Silda the manuscript while you were working on it? Because I can smell her tone a mile away. And if I can, you bet that Mom can too.

BROOKE *(defensive)* Yes, I did. She was there for a lot of it.

TRIP Yeah, she sure was, which she uses like a goddamn baseball bat to hit Mom and Dad with how crappy they were to Henry. What do you think Polly is gonna do to her sister when she realizes that Silda was goddamn Deep Throat for you?

BROOKE I needed someone else's eye to—

TRIP *(over her)*   Brooke, I'm just saying that you've made the story better and added a lot of very specific detail to show you as the victim. You and Henry. That doesn't mean you're a liar.

BROOKE   Then please, please Trip, just back me up. They listen to you before all others. Really. If you just said 'it's okay, it's okay', in that way you have. Because I'm not going to back down, I won't do it and they're going to have to learn to live with it. *(beat)* Please. Trip.

TRIP *(grinning)*   So, wait. Here are *my* assignments for Christmas: I have to get Mom not to send Silda out onto an ice-flow like some Eskimo, which will be her first instinct, and also get them to give you their blessing to publish a book, which paints them as right-wing sociopaths whose ideology destroyed their children's lives? Who am I? Rudolph the goddamn reindeer?

She suddenly laughs. It's that thing where siblings shift out of the real tension they're locked in and become kids again. Trip is grinning.

BROOKE *(suddenly laughing)*   You do have a shiny nose.

TRIP   I am sooo rolling a joint.

He proceeds to do this. Expertly.

BROOKE   You don't understand this depression thing because you don't have it.

There is a moment. He looks at her. He nods. Expertly rolling the joint through the following.

TRIP   Yeah, that's what *all* depressives say. How would *you* know what I have and don't have? How? You have your head so far up your own butt, you wouldn't notice if I were covered in killer ants and being stung to death right in front of you.

BROOKE   Don't say that.

TRIP   I mean, *it's true!* Oh, we joke about you not watching my show but it's *what I do, I make TV shows, it's part of my life,* my life.

(laughs, rueful) There are some things you don't know about me; I was impotent for a year, I developed an unhealthy relationship to sleeping pills and kicked it cold turkey. I dated a Russian woman almost twice my age and loved her. I take flying lessons and I happen to have read almost every book written about the Civil War.

BROOKE   You take *flying lessons?*

TRIP   Just because I am wasting my goddamn Stanford-Berkeley education making ironic and cheerful TV shows, doesn't mean *I'm not very, very much filled with despair.* Nobody who takes pleasure as seriously as I do could possibly be happy. Don't you know that? *(beat)* Look at me: I don't take my romantic life at all seriously. I am probably a sex addict. I don't want kids because it's far too easy to fuck them up, and our parents call me every time they need help with their e-mail or cell phones, and I am *presiding* over them getting older and parts are gonna start falling off of them and you haven't even noticed that Dad has a little invisible hearing aid which he is too vain to discuss—and they are the only people aside from you and Sleeping Beauty over there—*(nods toward Silda)*—that I have *ever* really, really loved, and *you're* half insane and vaguely suicidal. Silda is *entirely* insane and incapable of taking care of herself, and I can feel *myself* turning into Hugh Hefner. Welcome to the end of the goddamn Golden State. I am California! And California is not happy! *(Beat. Finished rolling, he offers her the joint.)* Have some.

BROOKE   *(taking a hit)*   Thank you. And I am not 'vaguely suicidal'.

TRIP   *(suddenly pissed at her)*   Well you could have fooled me, Brooke! What is it? Isn't it revenge enough that everyone worries about you all the time?

BROOKE   I hate that people worry about me—

TRIP   *(over her, laughing)*   No, you don't! Come ON! You love it! You had to add this book to it?

BROOKE But you told me I had to get back to work! You said it was up to me, that 'nobody was waiting for the next Brooke Wyeth novel'. And that I had to change that! I had to force myself on the world.

TRIP I said that to get you moving again. To get you writing. But not *this*. Besides, I thought you should write a nice goddamn *play* that nobody would ever go *see*!

BROOKE *(snaps)* You think I should put it in a drawer, don't you? Wait until they're gone! Jesus, just say it if that's what you think!

TRIP You want me to tell you what to do?

BROOKE God yes. Please! Please tell me what to do, I'll listen.

TRIP You never listen to anybody, but okay. *(flat)* If you're going to go ahead, do it without apology or drama, close your eyes and go for it—and if you're not, do it with grace and humility, how's that? I don't know! *(Beat. Suddenly really mad)* Just quit torturing everyone and looking at me like a lost *border terrier*, fuck!

BROOKE Stop trying to make it harder for me.

TRIP Why not? This should be the hardest decision you've ever made! *(Beat. Quietly, really upset)* They've been really good to you, Brooke, they've—you know they love you, they worship you, they think about you all day, they really love you so fucking much, you know that right?

He really takes her in. He shakes his head.

TRIP *(cont.)* I mean, this will sort of kill them. Doesn't that count in this life? Not withstanding whatever may have happened in the past, doesn't that count?

She looks at him, wishing he could go further, wishing he had something to offer her. But he can't.

SILDA *(suddenly awake, frantic)*   Jesus, I smell pot! I fell asleep here, oh my god, I'm so groggy! What time is it? Did you go to the club without me, goddamn it?

BROOKE *(calming)* It's eight-thirty, nobody's gone anywhere. Mom and Dad have not emerged from their quarters yet.

SILDA   They haven't?

Silda wraps the throw around her shoulders and gets up from the sofa, stands by the fire, warming herself.

SILDA *(cont.)*   You don't look so great, what, you've been crying? Did something happen? Did I miss—

BROOKE *(over her)*   No. We're just sitting here, you know, talking, waiting.

SILDA   Waiting for judgement day. Give me that joint.

TRIP   Oh yeah, that'll really help things; *you, high.*

SILDA *(as though he were a moron)*   I'm not allowed to drink, nobody said anything about drugs! Give it!

BROOKE   No. You have to keep your wits about you. Trip thinks Mom is going to make a thing about you looking at the manuscript. It will be construed in a particular way.

SILDA   Of course it will! Exactly! That's why I want the pot! I knew one day it would all come to a head. They're going to cut me off! Kick me out! Where will I go? There were no royalties for those goddamn stupid *Hillary* movies! I have social security, that's it, that's all. I'll end up in . . .

She stops. Polly is standing in the doorway.

POLLY   Where will you end up my darling? The Actors Home? If you're lucky, if you're very lucky. Perhaps some little stucco place in Desert Hot Springs? A retirement hotel? But we can get to that in due course, we can get to that later.

SILDA *(grabs the joint from Trip, and takes a drag)*   Oh boy.

Polly enters, manuscript in hand. Red-rimmed eyes.

POLLY *(infinite sadness)*   It's eight-thirty. If you like, we can still go to the club, have dinner. I could use a drink first, of course.

She crosses to the drinks tray and pours herself a liberal scotch, soda, rocks, from the ice bucket.

BROOKE   I don't think anyone's hungry.

TRIP *(grinning, slightly stoned)*   I'd like some M&M's or something . . .

BROOKE   We should talk. Where—where's Dad?

POLLY   In his study. He refused to read it. He refuses to take a position that might hurt you. Isn't that something? *(beat)* You know what I believe in?

SILDA *(she can't help it)*   Aside from the right to bear arms?

Polly takes the joint out of Silda's hand and puts it in the fireplace. She holds up the manuscript.

POLLY   Loyalty. Reciprocity. Brooke, from what I have read, from what I could bear to read, this is fiction.

BROOKE   Is it? Really?

POLLY   As a novel, it might be fun. Wicked. Nasty, smart, funny, sad, all those things. I have to admit. And kudos to your silent co-author here; my sister, the betrayer.

TRIP *(so tired of this shit)*   Oh, for God's sake, mom, let *that one go*, really, that's nothing, okay, please?

SILDA *(sober and weary and kind)*   Polly. Let it go; aren't you tired? What do you think you're protecting? The *Life* magazine picture of this family? Nobody remembers that! *Life* magazine folded years ago! *(infinite weariness, she shakes her head)* Honey: Nobody's looking. Nobody's watching anymore, sis. Nobody even reads anymore anyhow. This book? It's not nasty, it's even loving. More loving than I could've pulled off.

POLLY Of course you have a vested interest, I could hear your patois, your cadence, a mile off. So. I was wondering. Be honest with me. Please, for once. No lies. Is that it? Is it? *That's* why you started drinking again. Your consultations with my daughter?

SILDA *(laughing)* Hey. I didn't need a reason to drink, everyone else gets to escape in this place but me! Look at you! You guys are drunk by sundown!

POLLY Silda. I am so tired of worrying about what you might do next, about when you're going to take that final long drink of gin, I lost hope that you might be a loving sister to me before you *do* take that drink.

Silda laughs. She shakes her head.

SILDA Honey, I deserve a Nobel Peace Prize for loving you as much as I DO! How do you love someone *who became someone else?*

POLLY There are lots of bars open on Christmas Eve. I could even save you the trouble and pour you one myself.

SILDA *(quiet, smiles)* Oh, honey. By all means—do it. Here I am, sweetie, pour it, if you like; you offered. Go for it. *(beat)* And there it is: the real Polly Wyeth. In living color.

Silda points to Brooke.

SILDA *(cont.)* It's ALL in her book! *That's why you're being driven crazy by it!* Polly. I love you as much as I can, honey. But if you fuck your daughter over here the way you did Henry, I'll never let either of you live it down.

She has a smile on her face. She faces her sister, not backing down.

BROOKE So you're not going to sign off on this?

POLLY *(she turns to Brooke)*   Are you nuts? The entire thing is spurious. You've written an entire book based on the premise that we drove our son to suicide, but only after years of incubating him as a murderer. All these years, this is what you thought?

BROOKE   Then we have nothing left to say. I mean, I guess it was crazy to think you would be relatively okay with it. *(a sigh)* Well, I guess I must be as nuts as people say.

POLLY   Maybe you ARE! There's some manic energy in you *and* the book.

BROOKE   Oh, is that how you're gonna spin it, Mom? "I wrote the book while I was crazy"? You wanna go with that?

POLLY   Leaving aside the grotesque characterizations of various and sundry friends of ours who come across really as a parade of doddering, self-satisfied Paleolithic half-wits—

SILDA   Is that so far-fetched?

POLLY	**BROOKE**
Leaving that aside—	That is not what this is.

POLLY   Let me just read you an example. Let's see. *(reading)* "*After he is kicked out of the house Henry has not been seen in weeks. On the news, Chet Huntley is talking about an army-recruiting station in Long Beach that has been firebombed. The body of a janitor has been found inside, burnt beyond recognition.*"

Lyman enters the room. He stands listening. He is somewhat ashen. They stop.

LYMAN *(a low growl)*   Go on.

POLLY *(reading)*   *At two in the morning, there is shouting by the pool, Dad nose to nose with Henry, who is sobbing, pleading something. Without warning, Dad slaps him across the face with a retort that sounds like the tiny fireworks we used to buy in Chinatown. Again, two more times, Henry stock still as Lyman hits him again and again.*"

LYMAN *(suddenly)* Yes. He told me what he had been part of. I snapped. But I didn't stand there by our pool striking him repeatedly. It was a reaction—it was a reaction to this—

He stops. He hates doing this.

LYMAN *(cont.)* I am doing what I swore not to: I'm defending myself. Jesus.

POLLY *(reading)* *"By the time I get downstairs Henry is already gone. Dad looks at me, turns away and picks up the phone. Police cars are called. Henry is all over the news. Instead of looking for him, my parents have sent the LAPD to find him, no matter the consequences."*

And silence.

LYMAN *Of course* I called the police, I wanted him safe, in custody!

BROOKE *(looking down)* You may have wanted him safe, yes. But. You lost your temper and it wasn't the first time. *(beat)* There are reasons he made the choices he did.

LYMAN You see us as monsters?

BROOKE No, I don't, *but he did.*

LYMAN *(turns to Trip)* She presents us as ghouls who drove him to become some sort of murderer! *(back to Brooke)* Christ, there's something so vicious about what you're doing here, Brooke, don't you know that?

POLLY Of course not, she knows so little about actuality. The things she knows nothing about could fill the Library of Congress.

BROOKE Then tell me the things I don't know, I'll revise. When your son came to you for help, why did you slap him in the face and lose him forever?

LYMAN *(furious, and raging)* He was—he had rejected—he had *lost his mind.* *(beat)* Don't you understand what you're saying? The implication is that because I held that traditions, American traditions, should be protected from a generation of hooligans, including my own *son,* who had resorted to total chaos and who were mired in drugs and sex and nihilism and were going to destroy this country, I broke my son! It wasn't *politics* he was protesting, it was US! It was LIFE! He was ill, sick! Just like you, with a lot of anger just like you, and he had been a happy child, *just like you.* Do you remember how happy you were? Or is that a bit of convenient revisionism from us, too?

BROOKE *(emphatic)*   Until he was gone, I was. But not truly happy ever again.

LYMAN *(bitter, very, very bitter)*   Well—maybe you don't get to be happy for very long in this life.

BROOKE   Maybe. Maybe that's true, Dad.

There is silence. Somewhat shocked at his level of intense emotion at this. And then—

BROOKE *(cont.)*   I am so sorry but . . . I am suddenly so tired of the indentured servitude of having a family.

POLLY   Well, you're not going to have one for much longer, I'm afraid. *(beat)* I mean it. This is beyond repair. You insist that we publicly relive the worst time in our life, in a book and a magazine, and I am supposed to buckle because one is supposed to do anything for one's child, whatever one can to make them happy, to save them. THAT is indentured servitude.

BROOKE   Did you do that for Henry?

POLLY   You have no idea what we did for Henry. There are parts you don't understand, you were way too young.

BROOKE   Explain them then, you never have.

Lyman and Polly look at each other. She shakes her head, a warning.

LYMAN   If you understood what you were doing, you would hang your head in shame. I feel sick. I feel like this is a dream. I'm losing another child here! But I will never be able to . . . *(beat)* I

54

will never be able to love you again, I only had a little bit of my heart left intact after we lost Henry, and what's left is breaking, we'd be done as a family.

POLLY *(to Trip)*   Do you think she should publish it? How do you feel about it? What do you think?

Trip looks at them all.

TRIP   Yeah. You know, let me just like preface this with—uh, I've lived most of my life in the shadow of a brother I barely knew— and I have about *"this much"* left—okay? *(beat)* That said—the people in this book are not the same as the ones who brought me up. I've told Brooke this. They are different people than the ones I am looking at, totally.

Brooke looks stricken. She looks down at her feet, shakes her head. Polly nods, 'yes, exactly'. Trip looks at her.

TRIP *(cont.)*   But it's the best thing she's ever written.

SILDA   There. Listen to him!

POLLY *(a sharp stab)*   I see. So you think that as *literature*, it works, so therefore that tops all other concerns? Well that's simply quite frankly a morally despicable—

TRIP *(weary)*   I couldn't give a fuck about literature, Mom. I don't know the first thing about it. *(beat, and he goes forth without pause)* I say that we all live with each other's divergent truths and in spite of having deeply conflicting accounts, which don't matter anyway anymore—*(growing rage, finally it all comes out and it is scary)*— Because it's in the *past*! *(beat)* And we're all getting older and if this is heading toward desolation, which I can see it is, you will all regret it, so give your daughter a pass and your sister, too, both of you, stop fighting like weasels in a pit, because on your last day on this planet, you'll be scared and it won't matter as you take your last breath—all what will have mattered is how you loved. *(beat)* And I'm out. I'm done. That's all I got.

There is silence. He is spent and he exits.

POLLY   I can't. Not built for it. I know myself.

BROOKE   Yeah. Well then.

POLLY   I know myself.

SILDA *(with a quiet fury)*   That's right, Polly. *You. Know. Yourself.* Oh, you do. With such unyielding *certitude.* That's what your daughter has written. Her book is about two true believers. Who never let go.

She looks at her sister.

SILDA *(cont.)*   The zealots who have taken over your party and *marinated* it in intolerance. You guys let it happen. You are incapable of speaking out, even while finding fault with it in private. *(beat)* And you live in that complicity every day. A war in which so many people are dying in a desert, thousands of miles away. *Because* it's a war declared by a man whose father is someone with whom you occasionally *dine,* you keep silent. *That* is what true believers do. That, *that's* what your daughter has written.

POLLY *(a slow ironic clapping)*   Well. That's a good speech. All that liberal sentiment.

SILDA   Not liberal. Human.

POLLY   But I know that Henry came to you for help. And you were too drunk up there in Laurel Canyon to come down. *(beat)* I may be a true believer but at least I am not a hypocrite. To moralize, whine and moan, but when push came to shove, you weren't there for Henry. *He called you.* And you just were too busy in your wallow. And that is the story of Silda Grauman, who spent her life in the cheap seats telling us what shits we were, and who couldn't do anything to help someone she loved more than anyone in the world.

And Silda looks aghast.

BROOKE   He came to you, Silda?

SILDA *(helpless)*   I was—it was a very bad time and there was . . .

She stops, she can't say anything.

BROOKE   He came to you? Why did you not tell me that?

POLLY   Because it was not convenient to her fantasy of moral outrage, Brooke. That is why.

BROOKE *(almost horrified)*   But you sat there on the phone with me, giving me notes—

SILDA   I know.

BROOKE   We poured over those pages together, you sat there telling me what I had right—

SILDA *(desperate)*   But what you have IS right—you're in a very fragile state, you're—

POLLY *(vicious)*   Yeah, she didn't feed you that bit of info, did she, for your book, Brooke? Yeah, she left that out. So, you don't know the whole story.

BROOKE *(turning to Silda)*   Why would you not have told me?

POLLY   Because it was not convenient to her fantasy of moral outrage, Brooke. That is why.

SILDA   Polly, I know you, this is your way of—

POLLY   My way of pointing out the facts?

SILDA   Brooke, don't let her confuse the—

BROOKE   But this happened?

SILDA   There are—yes he—I think I told him that if he could get up to my house—I remember there were so many people at that house, it was a—he never showed up . . .

BROOKE *(almost horrified)*   But you sat there on the phone with me, giving me notes—

SILDA I know—

BROOKE *(she can't fathom this)* We *poured* over these pages together, you sat there telling me what I had right—

SILDA *(desperate)* But what you have IS right—you're in a very fragile state, you're—

BROOKE *(over her, with rising anger)* I'm fine—

SILDA Yes, he called me but don't let her sew doubt with—

BROOKE With what? With a *fact*?

SILDA I wanted to tell you—I don't care if you—you throw me in with everyone else—I at least know I failed—

POLLY *(vicious)* Yeah, she didn't feed you that bit of info, did she, for your book, Brooke? Yeah. She left that out. So. You don't know the whole story.

Lyman holds out his hand, trying one last time to walk back this catastrophe.

LYMAN *(a hoarse croak)* Brooke. Can't you please, please trust us? Wait. Publish it in a few years. Wait. That's all. Just wait 'til we are gone.

POLLY *(pouring scotch)* Which should only be a matter of hours, the way things are going.

BROOKE *(after a moment, ice cold)* Yeah. No. I'm not going to do that. You are asking me to shut down something that makes me possible. Your arguments for suppression mean I would die. Well, I've been dead before and I'm not going back. If it means that we're over, well, then it means we're over, and life will go on, one way or another. *(beat)* Dad, you're not even against—your *only* cohesive argument against the book is *not* that it's meretricious, but that I should wait for you to *die* before *publishing* it. Maybe it was crazy of me to try and write it, but I did. So, I owe myself more than that, and I owe Henry *a lot* more. You are asking that I help you? Henry asked *you* for help. He made a terrible, brutal, awful mistake and you shunned him. And with that, you have to live. *(beat, unyielding)* Relationships are hard-earned things; they have a reason and a logic to them. Well, I cannot go backwards into my cave. *(beat)* Mother, when you criticize and find fault in every last choice I make, for some reason, that's how you were made, and I know you tell yourself that it's because you're pushing me, you only want the best for me. *(beat)* You make it almost impossible for me to see the love in that. All I see is a bully who has lost touch with gentleness or kindness. That is what I see; there are many other ways of being. And yours, I just fail to understand it.

Brooke looks right at Polly. When Brooke says the next thing, Polly flinches. It is not cold or bitter, just fact.

BROOKE *(cont.)*   I. Can't. Bear. You. We have *earned* that relationship. That is the relationship we have earned, it is entirely organic, so no, I will not wait. I cannot—because I'm *just* like you: I know who I am. Most people don't have to make a step-by-step decision to stay alive, most people just basically want to live. I am not one of those people, not after Henry. *(beat)* There *will* be a book. Maybe it will be the last thing I ever publish, but there will be a book. It is the last six years of my life on those pages. And it's for Henry. I have no choice. What happened to Henry will have been seen. Everything. Everything in life is about being seen, or not seen, and eventually, everything IS seen. I am as sorry I am a writer as you are. I wish I had been made differently. But as it stands, I am . . . *(beat, a breath)* going to pack. And fly back east. And I will be home . . . *HOME* . . . by tomorrow evening. And in a few months, it will be out.

She starts to exit.

LYMAN   Brooke! Don't! You don't understand!

BROOKE	**LYMAN**
(a laugh)	Brooke, really, I—
What is there left to say, really?	
Dad? Maybe we'll—	

He turns to his wife, shaking his head.

LYMAN *(cont.)* I can not do this anymore, Polly! I can't. I just can't.

POLLY Don't. Don't. Really. Lyman.

LYMAN *(a great roar from him)* You know what, Polly? If I have to go on one more second keeping secrets, I'd rather live *alone*. I swear to you, I love you, but I would rather live alone. Than have one more second of this—

BROOKE *Of what?*

Beat. He stops. He looks at his wife. She is startled. Riven, motionless. She nods. She turns to Brooke.

POLLY *(a whisper)* Sit down. Please.

Trip and Brooke comply. Polly thinks for a moment. Lyman looks to Polly and nods.

POLLY *(cont.)* I was taught by Nancy, who was like a big sister to me—that to control everything, every bit of information, every gesture, every pose, that was the way to live. Order. Precision. Discipline. Well . . . *(beat)* every few years, someone from the Justice Department will come to see us. After all, he was never found. Suspicions remained and the case of Henry Wyeth remains open. A boy implicated in such a thing; the bombing of a recruiting center, a crime for which three other people are still in prison. And these visits always go the same. "Has there been any contact from anybody trying to get in touch with your son?" And have you ever heard from him, and does your phone ever ring and does the other party hang up after a moment without saying a word? Do you hear breathing on the other end of the line?

She stops. She looks to Lyman. "I can't do this alone."

LYMAN *(quietly)* We had been fighting. For a solid five years straight. Since Henry was fifteen and he became aware of the fact that we, his parents were on the wrong side. Of everything. All of it. And

I was not just an agent of the old guard but one of *it's spokesmen,*
and was for the war, and our fighting became more bitter, more
personal, and we lost him, the way you lose people you love. *(beat)*
And he moves to some squat in Venice, where the entire lifestyle
consists of drugs and screwing and there's not even a shower, and
we see less and less of him. *(beat)* I am helpless. Nobody knows
what to do. By now we are afraid of young people. The people in
his house are some sort of religionless theologians of liberation,
whatever they call themselves, but one day I open the *L.A. Times,*
and there's this story about a bombing, and this group in Venice
Beach is suspected and I knew. *(beat)* I remember it so clearly, he
shows up here, this filthy wraith, with long matted stringy hair,
and this filthy beard, and he's practically emaciated, and his eyes
are feverish and he's clearly ill—and he tells us. He tells us that he
didn't know. He had no idea. And he's crying, he's a boy again, and
I tell him he has to turn himself in, and he starts arguing *politics*
like a child, "but a man is dead," I yell, and he says "so are millions
of Vietnamese and Cambodians," and I slap him across the face
because I can't get through to him. And there's no coming back,
he looks at me, and . . .

Lyman stops. He shakes his head

LYMAN *(cont.)*   And he runs off, I run after him. And he's gone.

Lyman shakes his head, lost.

POLLY   It all comes out. He's in the papers. We're in the papers.
News people all over, going to our friends, camped outside. I
go numb, I don't care, I drive around town looking for him, all
over L.A. *(beat)* And then there he is, he somehow remembered,
he knew that once a week I volunteered at the Actors Home.
I was reading Dickens to ancient actors, most of whom were
deaf and blind, and I walk out to my car, and he's sitting in
the backseat. His clothes smell of that rancid ripe cheese,
homelessness, and he is really unrecognizable . . . *(beat)* It's a
straight drive up. You can do it in three days if you just keep
driving, almost all through the night, stopping for donuts and

coffee, coffee and—and who's going to stop a lady in a blue
Eldorado convertible and her clean-cut son? *(beat)* He cleaned
up so easily, with his hair cut, he still looked fifteen; gone was
the beard, gone were the rags, just put him in jeans and a Brooks
Brothers shirt and comb his hair and . . . it was so easy. At first
we didn't speak. Almost at all. And then he talked. Most of it,
still entirely self-deluded, at first, but finally, he just cried. "I have
blood on my hands now, too." *(beat)* "Everyone has blood on
their hands today." And more silence. Sleep. It was so easy, you
could just crossover, day trippers, really, before terror became
the . . . *(beat, disgust)* . . . . *profession* that it is today.

SILDA *(quietly)*   Oh my God. Oh my GOD.

LYMAN *(quietly, he can barely speak)*   And I took a plane up to Seattle.
So I could say goodbye, which we do. All three of us. On a ferry.
(beat) We sit in the car. We dictate his note. This suicide note. We're
crying. This apology. A night ferry, drop his old rags on the deck,
the deck of the ferry. Leave the note in his ragged shoes. On the
deck of this ferry. *(beat)* One of many ferries he will take. And I
hug him, the last time I will ever see him, of course, which we all
know. I will never see him again and I never have. *(Lyman starts to
cry)* And he said he was so so sorry and I said so was I. And I said,
"I will always love you, and we can never tell anyone about this"
and he said "but what about Brooke?" He asks us. "But what about
her?" *(a low moan escapes from Brooke)* And I said, "no child could be
expected to live with such a secret, and when the time is right we
will tell her, but there has to be some cost to what you were part
of. Maybe this is it." *(beat)* And, of course, it never came. The time
to tell you. I had no intention. I could have died then, I really didn't
care. Your mother insisted that I live. And that we thrive. *(beat)* So, I
get called to Bohemian Grove and I go, I host events, I have people
here, and I always think "if these men knew who I really was . . ."
But I can never show a trace of it. Because I think "if I can pass
as one of them, they will never know what I did." But acting, you
know, it's easy for me, it's easy. And I know he's alive, there's that, we

do know that, the phone, you know, it does ring. There IS a click. He is silent. He is there.

POLLY *(holds up the manuscript)*   The truth will out. *(a shrug, she looks at Brooke)* He is at risk at any time anyhow, always, the history, the secret history of the Wyeths' would be at terrible risk, all of your questions, all of your unanswered and unanswerable questions will turn on a light. In a closely guarded, carefully locked attic. Us in the papers again, old photographs of him, someone might recognize, and all of us guilty of this crime, this aiding and abetting. *(beat)* Now you know all the facts. Publish your book.

And Brooke is suddenly on her feet, and snatches the manuscript out of her hand and flings half of it at her father and half at her mother, and pages fly about, up into the air, hit the Wythes and drift to the floor.

BROOKE   I have spent years trying to—I have spent YEARS! YEARS! Of my life! In the fucking. . . *(a rush of words)* When I was in the hospital I tried to hold on and not kill myself because it would have been too much for you to have lost *two* children that way, and he gave me permission to do it, by having done it, he paved the way and I wanted to follow him! Every day I have to find my footing and not do—

LYMAN   BROOKE! *(fierce)* But you didn't! You haven't! You didn't die. And he's alive somewhere in this world! You are alive. And so are we! *(beat)* For a while longer at least. It is done. *(beat)* It is done. You. You are innocent, and you are kind, and you are, God knows, brave, and now you have to live with this knowledge too, and maybe one day you'll get to see him, probably . . . *(quietly)* *after* we're gone, but in the meantime, this is how we have lived, this is how we have managed to live. In this world. *(beat)* This world.

Lights fade.

Scene Two

March, 2010

Some suggestion, perhaps not literally, of Elliott Bay Bookstore in Seattle.

A book reading/signing. Brooke is finishing reading sections of Love & Mercy *to the crowd. Trip is there.*

BROOKE   Let's see. I'm skipping around a little. I have these sort of easy, bite-sized sections—this—is toward the end—*(She looks out smiling.)* God look at you all. I love Seattle. You love books here. I guess it's the rain, isn't it? *(A small laugh. Beat. She clears her throat. She reads)* Lyman died on a weekend. One of those absurd and overly cinematic ocher and umber Palm Springs sunrises after a feverish, morphine clouded night. It took a few minutes. He had a conversation with himself, or with an imaginary director, on a long forgotten set, about whether or not he needed another take. He once made a list for me of his death scenes, and there were many of them, perhaps fifty. And now he was really having one, but of course, dementia deprived him of the real deal. For him, it would only be Hollywood. He was lost to the movies. His first love, I suspect. He insisted that he in fact, needed another take. In this hallucination of his, my mother and I sat, and listened. He could do better, he told the director. He had another take in him. *(a laugh)* Ever was it thus. *(beat)* And Polly and I sat by the pool.

She stops reading and smiles.

BROOKE *(cont.)*   Which is what we did best for the rest of her life. After I moved in next door. But of course, if you buy the book, if you are *gullible* enough to buy my book, you can read about that. The—fun with her. It—no—it actually ended up—

She shakes her head.

BROOKE *(cont.)*   We got to know—each other in that way—when all the men are gone, suddenly, and—*(She looks down at her copy of her book)* Let's see—one little—thing here—I marked it, but

I seem to have lost all my places—God, people used to ask me when my next book was coming out—*(beat, a smile)* I mean, because it had been announced and then it never came out, and—anyway, it took a long time to do that thing of stepping away, and looking at it all from some distance—distance is always good . . . My brother Trip, who is here tonight, tells me that I tend to run long, so I'll wrap it up with a little thing about our late brother Henry.

Beat. A Bright smile. She laughs. She is happy.

BROOKE *(cont.)*   Here it is. *(reading)* "Henry is showing me a short cut through the backyards of Bel Air, and he is expert, at fourteen, tan and stealthy, a subversive, knows where fences have holes in them, knows where there are no fences, knows where trees can be climbed, and he is ahead of me, his long hair, his multicolored jeans flashing between the leaves of lush Bel-Air Jacaranda trees, and he is beckoning me to follow him, but I am losing him, I am not as fast as he is. I am not as fast, not as brave, not as adventurous, not as easy with neighborhood dogs, not as fearless . . . *(beat)* And he turns around to wait for me for one moment, while hanging on the branches of a tree over a long white wall that separates the seclusion of Bel Air from Sunset Boulevard, and he can wait no longer. And he drops from the tree, on the other side of the wall, and I think . . ." Now he is gone. How will I find him . . ."

Brooke closes the book. She looks out at the audience, smiling.

BROOKE *(cont.) (a small laugh)*   How will I find him?

She smiles, and looks out at the crowd. Making contact with the audience, watching . . .

THE END